Giulio BRICCIALDI

The Carnival of Venice
(Il Carnevale di Venezia, Op. 78)
for Flute and Piano

Edited, Arranged and Performed by
SIR JAMES GALWAY

NOTE

Please see back page of this part
for practice and performance notes.

Southern
MUSIC

Il Carnevale di Venezia
for Flute and Piano
Op. 78

Flute

G. Briccialdi
Edited, arranged and
performed by Sir James Galway

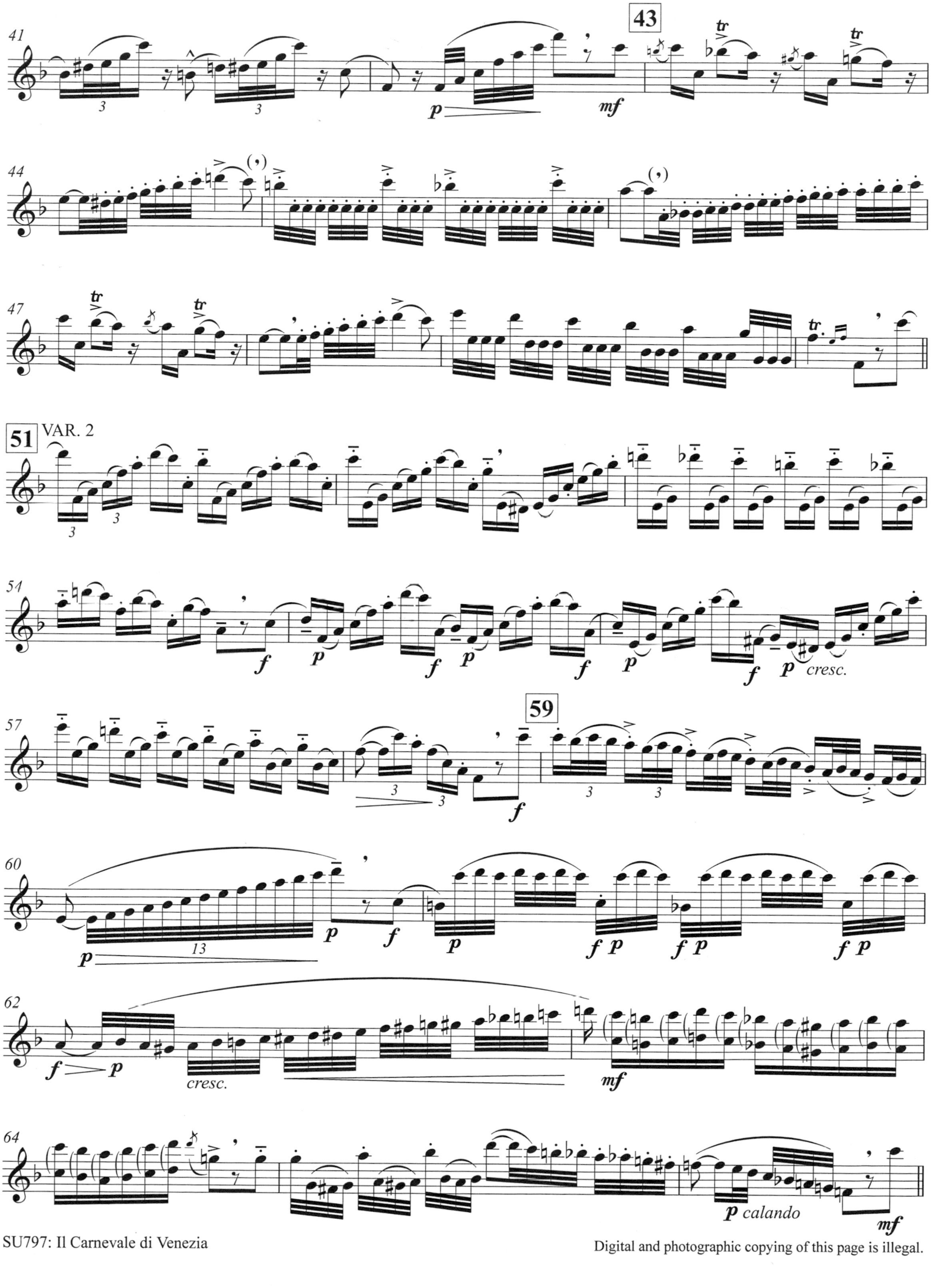
43
VAR. 2
51
59
cresc.
calando

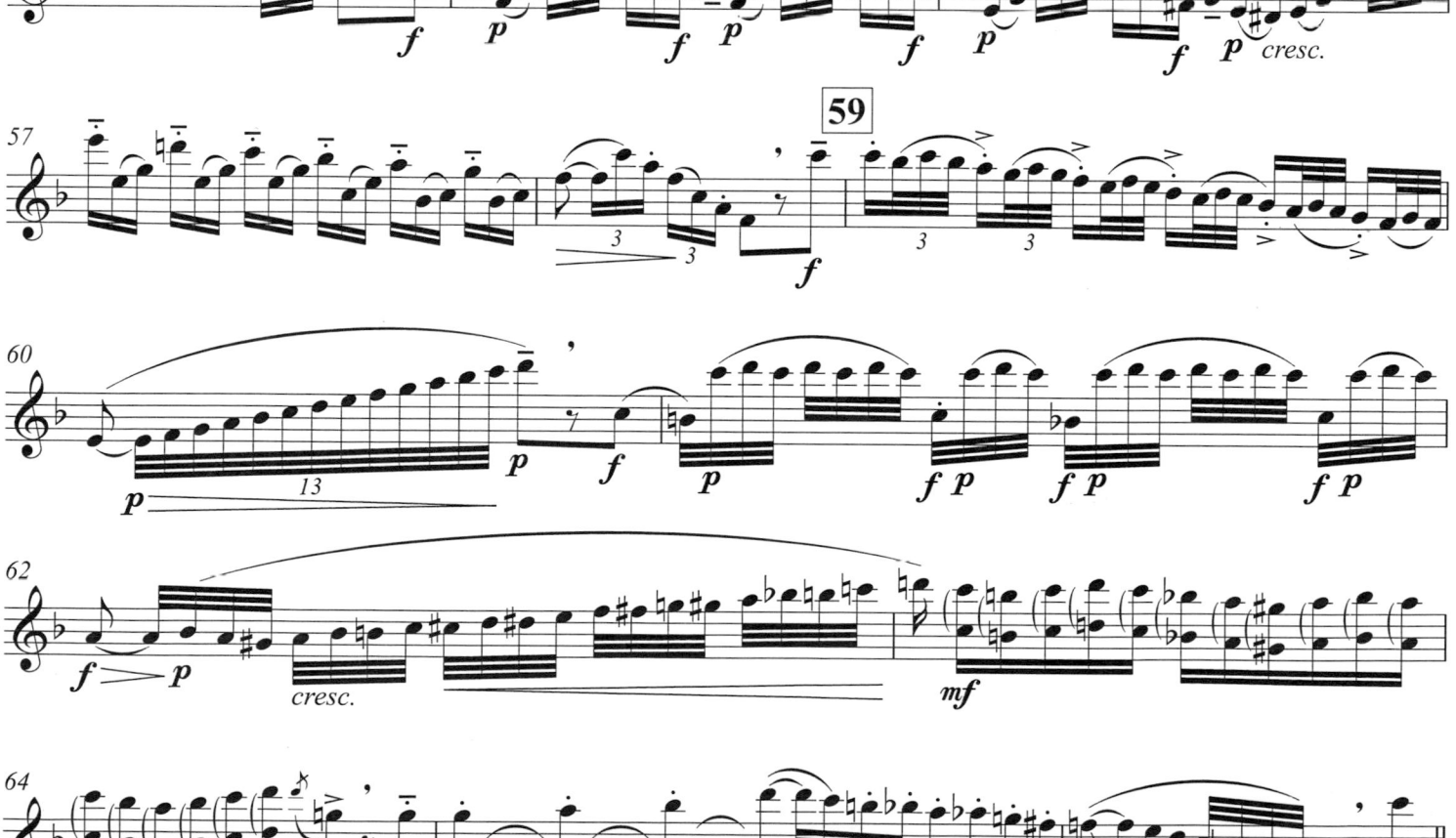

Flute

Flute

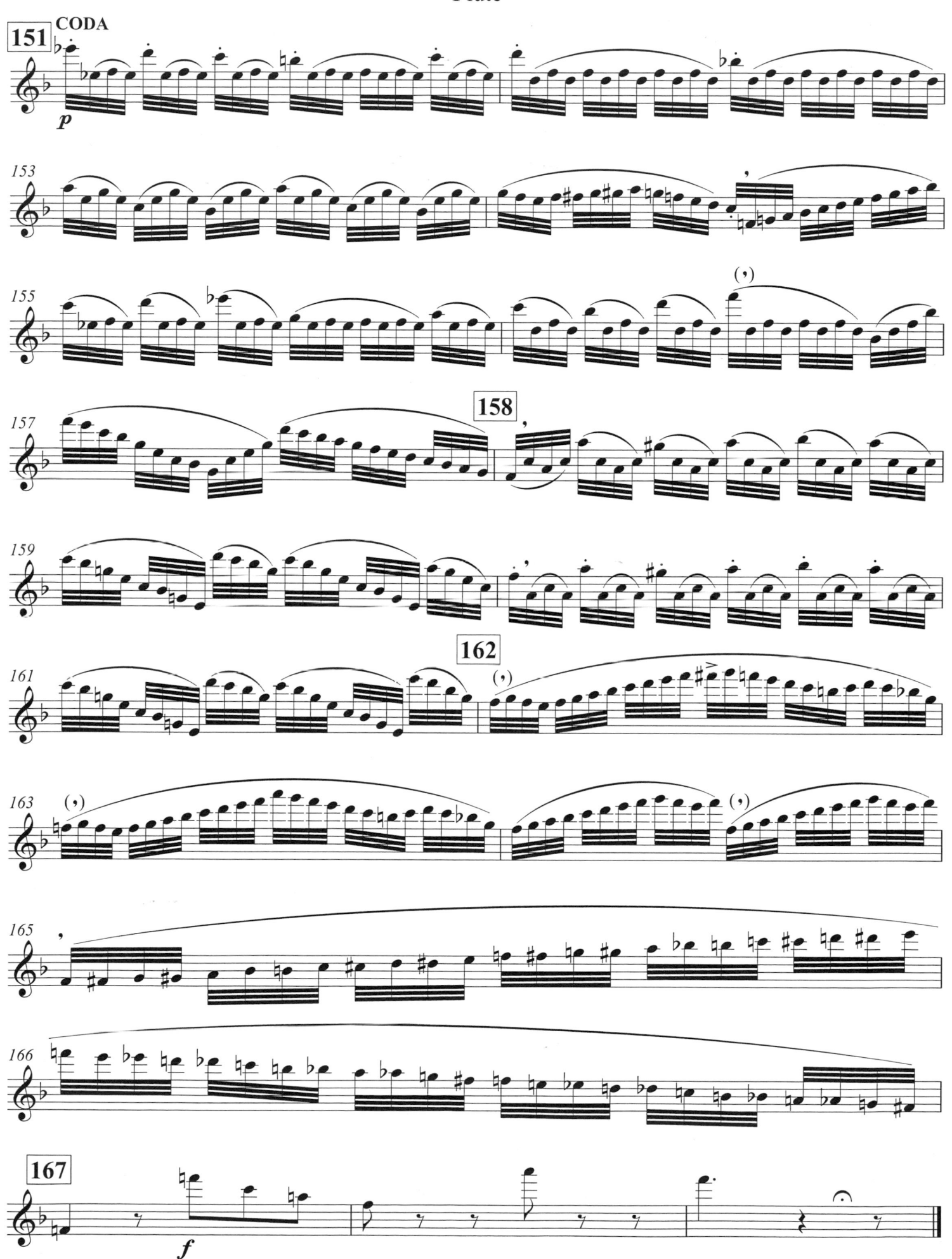

Il Carnevale di Venezia Op.78 for flute and piano—Performance notes by SIR JAMES GALWAY

This piece contains an introduction, theme, seven variations and a coda. The following are my recommendations to playing the piece:
- Pay attention to the speed of each variation. They should all be slightly different.
- Try to bring out the melodic material at all times.
- Learn to take quick short breaths without opening the mouth too much.
- Feel free to use the B flat lever throughout the piece. After all, it was written by the man who invented this most useful key.
- What we want to avoid is repetition of expression throughout the piece.

INTRODUCTION: In the introduction and in the theme, I would recommend employing a nice Italian singing style. This means giving full projection to the melody and to the notes at the end of phrases. Don't cut short the notes at the end of the phases. I have put a line above notes I think should be long. This will give you time to employ a good singing style. Briccialdi, the composer, uses the sign " > " not to indicate an accent, but to indicate playing the note little bit longer to give more expression.

In bar 11, I have inserted a piano sign in order to indicate this part should be played soft and singing. In bars 17 and 18, I have inserted this sign " | " to indicate taking a little extra time between the flute note and the piano chord. The last note should be played a little longer to introduce the theme.

ALLEGRETTO: Generally, the notes with dots should not be played too short. Remember, it is only *staccato* not *staccatissimo*. Try in bar 31 to play with your best low register tone.

VARIATION 1: Here you want to play the melody with a good singing projection. The tempo for this little variation should be decided by the speed at which you can play bars 44 through 49. Here the breathing is very important, too. Try not to open your mouth too much as you need to be careful forming the embouchure after the breath. And the more open your mouth is, the more you have to correct the embouchure when you come back to play after the breath.

VARIATION 2: Again, I would recommend a tempo that will give you time to play all the notes beautifully and with a good expression. You will need to play some of the notes a little bit longer to bring out the melody, and here I have indicated them with a " - ". In bar 61, use your trill key to play the 32nds and in bar 63, I think it is easier to play the top note of the octaves first.

VARIATION 3: This is one of the most famous of all the variations. Here, we have to take care the melody is clearly stated and the accompaniment as soft as you can safely manage.

Here, I would like to say a word regarding general practice. It is not enough to play through a variation with impression that you have it under your fingers after playing through the piece two or three times. It is more beneficial to play these parts which are really difficult at least 10 times each, every day. The breathing in this variation is particularly difficult and I have marked where I breathe. You can adopt a slightly quicker tempo in this variation. In bar 75, just play a tad slower, as in variation 4 we are going to play a little quicker.

VARIATION 4: In this creation you get to show off your F major scales and arpeggios. You can play this one a little bit quicker than the last variation. In bar 91, let us hear your best low register. Here again, I must remind you to practice your low notes. After all, you want to be able to impress the listeners and present the composer at his best.

VARIATION 5: Relax the tempo in this variation in which Briccialdi gives you a chance to shine. Here you want to play with your very best tone giving your listeners a break from F major. In the very first bar, make sure the little notes are the best you can manage. And in bar 107, begin to push the tempo a little bit going to 110, where you can insert a little *rubato* taking up the tempo again at 111. At the end of bar 113, you can make a little *rallentando* to finish the phrase off nicely. This next little episode, bars 122 to 126 needs great care with the trills. They should all be fast. Here I would recommend practicing the Boehm *Caprice no. 5*. You don't need to learn the whole study, just bars 1–28.

This brings us to bar 126. Hold onto your to B flat, then take a breath and begin the scale. Don't start too slow, but slow enough that you can make an impressive *accelerando*. Change your embouchure as you go down the scale in order to arrive on a perfect low C. When you play a B-flat trill, pull down the index finger of the right hand. This means that while trilling with the thumb, you are only tilling with one key instead of two keys.

VARIATION 6: The tempo of this variation will depend on how fast you can play bars 130 and 133. I recommend you practice these two bars until you can play them fast and flawlessly. Bar 137 gives you a chance once again to show off your trills followed by a chromatic scale which should be played strictly in tempo.

VARIATION 7: The success of this variation depends on the flexibility of your embouchure. Try your best with the little notes. It might be worthwhile to practice this variation a little slower so you can discover what is required of your embouchure.

CODA: This little coda is very difficult for the breathing. You might want to consider how you take a quick breath. My recommendation is that you don't open your mouth so much. Opening the mouth more than necessary brings with it added difficulty of finding a good embouchure for the note to be played directly after the wide-open mouth breath.